W9-ANQ-807

SRA Early Interventions in Reading

Kids with Great Ideas

By
Hilary Mac Austin

Illustrated by
Lyle Miller

SRA

Columbus, OH

The **McGraw·Hill** Companies

Photo Credits

7 ©Raymond Kleboe/Getty Images, Inc.

MHEonline.com

SRA

Imprint 2012

Copyright © 2005 by SRA/McGraw-Hill.

All rights reserved. Except as permitted under the United
States Copyright Act, no part of this publication may be
reproduced or distributed in any form or by any means,
or stored in a database or retrieval system, without the
prior written permission of the publisher, unless otherwise
indicated.

Send all inquiries to:
SRA/McGraw-Hill
8787 Orion Place
Columbus, OH 43240-4027

Printed in China.

ISBN 0-07-604477-7

6 7 8 9 NOR 15 14 13 12

Contents

Chapter 1
Louis Braille

What would we do without inventors? They make our lives easier, and they make our lives more enjoyable. There are many famous inventors, but did you know it's possible for children to be inventors too? It's true. Children have accomplished many important inventions.

For example, have you heard of braille? Braille is writing for people who are blind. Louis Braille invented this system of writing.

Louis was only fifteen years old when he invented this sensible, ingenious writing. The writing system is in patterns of raised dots, and blind people "read" and distinguish these patterns with their fingers.

Louis was born in France in 1809, and he was three when he became blind. When he was ten, he went to Paris to a special school for people who were blind.

Because Louis couldn't use his eyes, he learned by listening and memorizing, but he wanted to read books too. At that time there were only a few books for people who were blind. These books had raised letters that were very large, which meant the books were humongous and heavy. It was almost impossible to read and finish these books quickly; it took a long time to read just one sentence.

One day a man came to Louis' school in Paris. The man had invented an admirable new kind of writing for soldiers that helped them read messages that weren't visible at night. The writing was raised dots on paper, with different patterns of dots standing for different sounds. The writing was a special code the man called "night writing."

The military decided not to use night writing, so the man thought of using his invention for people who were blind. Unfortunately, the students at the school didn't like the writing. It took too long to finish a sentence because the sounds in just one word took up too much space. Also, the code was terribly difficult to memorize.

Louis also didn't think night writing was feasible, but he was intrigued by the concept and began to create his own writing. He used patterns of raised dots, but the dots didn't stand for sounds and weren't shaped like letters. Instead, Louis invented an alphabet of ABCs in which all the letters were patterns of raised dots.

In the braille alphabet each letter is represented in a rectangular shape that resembles a domino. Each rectangle can have up to six raised dots, and each letter is a different pattern. Louis also created special patterns for numbers and punctuation marks. He even created patterns for writing music. This was incredible!

Besides his system of writing, Louis also invented a machine that prints braille. This machine, called the Raphigraph, made it possible to produce an incredible number of books in braille. Louis was tremendously advanced and ahead of his time. People all over the world continue to use his writing system even today.

Chapter 2
Chester Greenwood

Sometimes inventions are simple, and you might think, "Wow, *I* could have thought of that." For example, who thought of earmuffs? Chester Greenwood did, and he was only fifteen years old! Greenwood lived in Farmington, Maine, in 1873. The winters are terribly chilly in Maine, and Chester's ears wouldn't stay adequately warm. His ears would become cold and numb whenever he went outside.

One year Chester received a new pair of ice skates, and he couldn't wait to try them! He dressed to go out in the frigid winter air, wrapping his scarf over his ears. But the scarf didn't do a very good job, and Chester's ears became overwhelmingly cold. He wasn't having any fun, though he wasn't willing to give up and go inside just yet.

Chester decided to solve his problem. He formed two circles of wire and asked his grandmother to sew fur onto each circle. Then he attached a band between the circles. The band went across the top of his head and held the fur over his ears. He tested his sensible invention and was astonished: It worked!

Chester's ears remained warm! He called his invention "ear mufflers" because a scarf is also sometimes called a muffler. Today we say simply "earmuffs." Chester patented his invention, and later he adapted and improved it. Every head is a different size, and Chester wanted to make earmuffs that would fit every size. He also wanted to make his earmuffs easier to carry.

Chester created a new, adjustable headband that could be made longer or shorter. These new stylish earmuffs could fit every size of head. This is what "one size fits all" means. What an imaginative idea!

Chester went on to create another sensible improvement for his invention.

Chester made the steel in the headband coiled. That way, when the band went across the head, the band uncoiled and fit tightly. When the earmuffs were taken off, the band curled again and overlapped itself. Now people could keep their earmuffs in their pockets because the earmuffs were collapsible. These improved earmuffs were not only adjustable to every head, but they were also easy to carry.

Chester later named his earmuffs Greenwood's Champion Ear Protectors. He opened a factory, and as earmuffs became more popular, the factory grew. Chester relished inventing and kept at it as time went on. Overall, he invented a folding bed, a hook to lift doughnuts when they're still hot, a new spark plug for cars, and a rake with steel teeth.

However, Chester is most famous for his wonderful earmuffs. People's ears are warm in the winter, thanks to Chester's imagination.

People in Farmington are especially proud of Chester. Every December the town has a big parade to celebrate Chester's incredible accomplishments. During the parade, everyone in town wears earmuffs— even the dogs. There are also gigantic earmuffs for the police cars!

Chapter 3
Margaret "Mattie" Knight

Margaret Knight was another child inventor. Mattie was born in 1838, and she grew up in Manchester, New Hampshire. Mattie loved to build things. People called her a tomboy because back then only boys were supposed to like to build, but Mattie didn't care. Neither did her brothers, because Mattie built the most admirable sleds in town!

Mattie's family wasn't rich, so when she was ten years old, she went to work in the textile mill where her brothers worked. Because of this, Mattie didn't finish school. This wasn't unusual; many children didn't finish elementary school back then because they needed to earn money for their families. Overall, Mattie and many other children worked thirteen hours a day at the mill. It was hard and dangerous work.

A textile mill is a place where machines weave cloth; these machines are called looms. One important part of the loom is the shuttle, which holds the thread and moves back and forth across the loom very quickly. Some shuttles in the mill had pointed ends, and it was dangerous when a loom broke down because the shuttle could come off the loom.

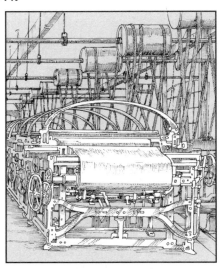

One day at the mill Mattie saw a horrible accident. A shuttle became loose on a loom and flew away from the machine, injuring a young worker. Mattie knew something had to be done. She had to fix this problem. She wished to make it so the shuttle would stay attached to the machine and so the machine would stop automatically when something went wrong.

Mattie made time after work each day to plan a way to achieve this. First she thought about what had to be done, and then she drew some sketches. Finally she built small models of her sketches. When she was done and the invention worked, she was quite pleased, and so was everyone else at the mill.

The invention was a stop-motion device, which means it automatically turned off the loom and stopped the shuttle from moving when something went wrong. Mattie never patented what she had accomplished; she simply gave her idea to the mill, because she wanted people to be safer as soon as possible. Soon her invention was being used in mills all over the country. And she was only twelve years old!

Just as Chester Greenwood continued inventing things throughout his life, Mattie continued to invent things as well. She patented almost thirty inventions including a special machine that created paper bags. The bags folded flat to make them easy to store. They also had flat bottoms so they were easy to carry and could hold more groceries. Then something astonishing happened— someone stole Mattie's idea!

In the end, Mattie had to go to court to prove she invented the paper-bag machine. She won her case. Mattie went on to invent machines that cut and sewed leather for shoes. She also invented parts for engines. She was a busy, responsible woman! She used her imagination, and she always had another new idea.

Chapter 4
Frank Epperson

Here's another great invention: the Popsicle! Many people love Popsicles because they taste great and keep us cool. Frank Epperson invented the Popsicle in 1905 when he was only eleven years old. You might think inventing the Popsicle would have been easy, because the Popsicle is just a frozen fruit drink. Anyone could have invented the Popsicle, right?

Actually, it was harder than you might think. In 1905 people didn't have the advantage of refrigerators or freezers to keep food cold or to make ice. In the winter, people cut ice from rivers and lakes and put the ice into a special container they called an icebox. Even with an icebox, it was hard to keep things cold because the ice always melted.

Frank Epperson lived in San Francisco, California. It doesn't get very cold there, so people there used to import ice from far away. If Frank didn't have ice or a freezer, how did he invent a frozen treat?

There are two versions of the story. The first version is that Frank's invention was a mistake: He stirred up a drink and accidentally left it outside overnight.

The second story is that Frank knew what he was doing. He liked inventing new fruit drinks, and one winter night he decided to try something original. He knew it was going to get miserably cold that night, so he left a drink outside with the stirring stick still in it. That night something incredible happened.

What was so amazing? It almost never freezes in San Francisco, but that night the temperature dropped below freezing. This was fortunate, because Frank's drink froze with the stirrer still in it. The next morning he removed the frozen treat from its container. He licked the treat, and it tasted good! But Frank couldn't do anything about his invention, because he couldn't figure out how to freeze something except by leaving it outside in a dish.

When Frank grew up, he married and had five children. He sold lemonade at fairs and amusement parks, but his family was still quite poor. Frank tried to think of ways to make more money. Then he remembered his frozen-drink invention. Making his frozen treat wasn't a problem because by then electric refrigerators and freezers had been invented. The time was right!

Frank thought his invention could be popular. He tried to find someone else who would manufacture his treats, but people told him his idea was misguided, wasn't feasible, and would never sell. That didn't stop Frank. He decided to do things himself. He invented a machine to freeze his treats, and he used test tubes as molds.

Frank established his invention and patented it in 1924. First he called his treat the Epperson Icicle, but too many people mispronounced the name, so he changed the name to the Epsicle. However, his children didn't call it an Epsicle—they called it "Pop's 'sicle." Frank liked that name better, so he renamed his treat the Popsicle.

At first, each Popsicle had just one stick. But in the 1930s many people were poor and couldn't afford Popsicles, so Frank invented the Twin Popsicle. The Twin Popsicle cost only a nickel and had two sticks, which meant that people could split it in half and share it. Frank later invented other frozen treats—the Dreamsicle, the Creamsicle, and the Fudgsicle— that many children still relish today.

Chapter 5
Krysta Morlan

Krysta Morlan is a young inventor in today's world. She invents things that help people with disabilities, and she has been very successful. Krysta was born with cerebral palsy, which means she can't use some of her muscles very well. Krysta's muscles sometimes spasm involuntarily, and this can make it hard to walk.

People with cerebral palsy sometimes have operations to improve their condition. When Krysta was in the ninth grade, she had a major operation on her legs. After the operation, she had casts on both her legs that went all the way from her hips to her ankles. She had to stay in bed while her legs were in the casts.

All summer Krysta recovered from her operation, and she was miserable. Her casts were hot. Her legs overwhelmingly itched all the time, and she couldn't scratch them. This was all extremely unpleasant, but Krysta didn't sit and cry. She decided to solve her problem. She thought about what would help her legs feel better in the casts. Krysta designed the Cast Cooler.

The Cast Cooler is an uncomplicated device made of a tube, a pump, and a battery. One end of the tube fits between the cast and the skin. The other end of the tube is connected to the pump. The battery runs the pump. Krysta used the pump from her aquarium because an aquarium pump normally pushes an overflow of air into water.

Krysta used the aquarium pump to send an overload of cool air down the small tube into her cast, next to her hot, itchy skin. The cool air inside the cast made her itch less and feel better, which was a lot more effective than just turning up the air conditioning.

The Cast Cooler wasn't all Krysta invented.

Eventually Krysta's casts came off, but her work wasn't finished. She hadn't moved her legs for a long time, and she needed special exercise, called physical therapy, every day to help her misshapen leg muscles learn to move, walk, and become flexible again. Even though she sometimes exercised in a swimming pool, it was boring, so Krysta decided to make it fun.

Krysta invented the Waterbike. Part of the Waterbike is above water, and part of it is underwater. The Waterbike works a little like a bicycle does, but it floats like a boat does. The person pedals the Waterbike like a bicycle, and the person's legs get the exercise they need. This is beneficial and effective therapy.

How does the Waterbike work? The pedals let the rider move the Waterbike around the pool, and a rudder makes it possible to steer so the person can control where he or she advances in the pool. The Waterbike also has fins for balance so it doesn't overturn. The whole bike is made of light plastic tubes and foam. This way the Waterbike doesn't sink!

The Waterbike is fun to ride, which helps make exercise fun. Physical therapy in the pool can feel like a game as the person pedals around in the water, all the while strengthening leg muscles and improving health.

When Krysta was a teenager, she became a successful inventor. Though she's older now, she continues to develop new ideas to help people with disabilities.

Chapter 6
Kavita Shukla

Kavita Shukla also lives in today's world, observing problems and thinking of ways to fix them. When she was thirteen years old, Kavita watched her mother pump gasoline into the car and then make the mistake of forgetting to put the gas cap back on the car afterward. Kavita saw a similar problem in her science class: Students continually forgot to put the lids back on bottles and test tubes.

The bottles had chemicals in them. Kavita imagined it would be very dangerous for scientists if they forgot to put the lids back on their bottles. If the bottles tipped over and chemicals were mixed together, there could possibly be a mishap and explosions. Kavita thought of a solution and invented a new lid. This lid reminds people to put the lid back on the bottle.

Kavita thought up a great name for her invention—the Smart Lid. If a scientist forgets to put the Smart Lid back on a bottle of chemicals, the lid beeps and lights. This reminds the scientist to put the lid back on, and the lab and scientists are safe from any potential explosions.

Kavita didn't stop there. She continued inventing, because she continued to see problems. The idea for Kavita's next invention came soon after she invented the Smart Lid. When she was in the seventh grade, she went to visit her grandmother in India. Some of the water in India isn't clean, and the bacteria can make people sick.

One day Kavita accidentally drank some contaminated water. She was afraid she would get sick, but Kavita's grandmother knew an old cure. She gave Kavita a spice called fenugreek. Fenugreek is often added to Indian cooking and is believed to kill bacteria. Kavita's grandmother's cure worked; Kavita didn't get sick.

Back home in the United States, Kavita wanted to find out how fenugreek works. She experimented and discovered that fenugreek works on water bacteria and on many other kinds of bacteria too. She also discovered that fenugreek works on molds. She learned that fenugreek makes some bacteria and molds grow more slowly.

One day Kavita took some strawberries from the refrigerator, but they were rotten. She was disappointed that the strawberries were inedible and was disappointed that the food had been wasted. *Too many people in the world need food for any to be misused,* she thought. Kavita remembered her experiments with fenugreek and wondered if fenugreek could possibly kill the bacteria that rot food.

She concocted a mixture of fenugreek and water, and then she added some paper, soaking it in her mixture. When the paper was dry, Kavita wrapped some food in it. Would the food rot as quickly as usual, or would the fenugreek in the paper help kill bacteria? The food stayed fresh longer! Food wrapped in her paper remained fresh four to six weeks longer than food without the special paper.

Without fenugreek paper

With fenugreek paper

Kavita's paper is natural, which is good for the environment; the paper is easy to manufacture, which is good for poor countries. The paper keeps food fresh longer, which is good for everybody.

Kavita received patents for her accomplishments and has also won many prizes. What will she think of next?

Chapter 7
Two Brothers

As you've learned by now, inventors can be any age. One boy was only eight years old when he invented something special for his mother. The boy's mother had a problem with her heart. Her heartbeat was too slow, so she had a pacemaker to help adjust the beats. A pacemaker is a small device that doctors put inside a person's chest.

A pacemaker has to be tested every week to make sure it's working properly and not destroyed. The boy's mother, however, didn't have to go to the hospital to do this test. Instead, she called the hospital on the telephone. The hospital tested her heartbeat over the phone! How is this possible?

Do you know about modems? Some computers use a modem to connect to the Internet. The boy's mother wore a special bracelet that could be connected to a modem as well. The bracelet read the pulse in her wrist and then sent her pulse electronically to a machine at the hospital, where doctors looked at the measurements.

Unfortunately, sometimes the bracelet didn't work dependably. The boy's mother had thin wrists, and the bracelet slipped frequently. This broke the electrical connection. The boy and his mother tried many ways to make the bracelet work better. The boy held the bracelet tightly to his mother's wrist, and his mother put water on her wrist. Water made the connection stronger.

Yet the bracelet still didn't work very well, so the boy decided to invent something better. He put an elastic band on the bracelet, which made the bracelet fit tighter. Then he attached sponges soaked in electrolytes. Electrolytes are special chemicals in our bodies—chemicals we need to stay replenished and healthy.

The boy had an electrolyte solution at his house that was for his pet lizard; even lizards need electrolytes. Why did the boy use an electrolyte solution? He knew electrolytes help with electrical connections better than plain water does. The boy's special sponges made the bracelet work more reliably. It was the perfect solution!

This eight-year-old boy had a brother who was six years old. The younger brother wanted to invent something as well. When he went to the hospital with his mother, he saw many patients who were young children. They didn't seem to be too delighted, and he wished to help them feel better.

When people are sick, sometimes they're given IVs. An IV is a way to give medicine; *IV* stands for *intravenous,* which means "into the vein." A bag of medicine is attached to a small tube, and the tube goes into a person's arm through a needle. Some IVs are hooked to tall poles with wheels so people can walk and won't be deprived of medicine.

The younger brother saw the children in the hospital walking with their IV poles, and he thought of an idea. His idea was to attach IV poles to small toy cars. This way children could ride around in the cars and receive medicine through their IVs at the same time.

These two creative, responsible brothers thought of delightful, helpful ideas. Many other children have ideas just as delightful. How about you?